OLYSLAGER AUTO LIBRARY

British Cars of the Early Thirties 1930-1934

compiled by the OLYSLAGER ORGANISATION

edited by Bart H. Vanderveen

FREDERICK WARNE & Co Ltd
London and New York

THE OLYSLAGER AUTO LIBRARY

This book is one of a growing range of titles on major transport subjects.
Titles published so far include:·

The Jeep
Cross-Country Cars from 1945
Half-Tracks
Scammell Vehicles
Tanks and Transport Vehicles of World War 2
Fire-Fighting Vehicles
Earthmoving Vehicles
Wreckers and Recovery Vehicles
Passenger Vehicles 1893–1940
Buses and Coaches from 1940
Fairground and Circus Transport

American Cars of the 1930s
American Cars of the 1940s
American Cars of the 1950s
American Trucks of the Early Thirties
American Trucks of the Late Thirties

British Cars of the Early Thirties
British Cars of the Late Thirties
British Cars of the Early Forties
British Cars of the Late Forties
British Cars of the Early Fifties
British Cars of the Late Fifties

Motorcycles to 1945

Copyright © Olyslager Organisation NV 1973
Reprint with revisions 1975

Library of Congress Catalog Card No 73-75032

ISBN 0 7232 1711 4

Filmset and printed in Great Britain
by BAS Printers Limited, Wallop, Hampshire

753.1075

INTRODUCTION

Internationally speaking, British cars of the early thirties formed a class of their own, and a most interesting one. On the one hand there were the little economy cars, exemplified by the legendary Austin Sevens and Morris Minors, and at the other extreme were some of the world's most desirable luxury cars such as the Rolls-Royce, Bentley, Alvis and Daimler, to name but a few. There were also the rather unorthodox designs of Morgan and Trojan and the irresistible and unique sports cars, produced by small factories like Aston-Martin, Frazer-Nash, Lagonda and MG. On the export front it was often these unique cars which sold relatively well, there being little overseas competition. Imports were low, mainly because of the crippling horse-power tax which plagued the British public, but helped to keep balance of payment figures at bay. This system of taxation had commenced in 1921 and private cars with engines exceeding six horse-power were taxed at the rate of £1 per horse-power, calculated on the Royal Automobile Club's formula which only took cylinder bore into consideration. It was founded upon an assumed piston speed of 100 ft/min and a mean effective pressure of 90 lb/sq.in with a mechanical efficiency of 75 per cent. This was purely hypothetical and many of the engines of the early 1930s developed several times the taxable horse-power. The formula for obtaining the RAC rating was: $HP = \dfrac{D^2 n}{2 \cdot 5}$ where D equalled the bore in inches and n the number of cylinders. This system, wherein the piston stroke was not taken into account, was used until after the second World War.

The old method of taxation put a heavy premium on owning a car with an engine larger than was absolutely necessary and encouraged manufacturers to produce engines with a small bore and a long stroke, with the result that the average British cars most in demand on the home market were of 10 HP and lower ratings. Understandably this had a detrimental effect on exports, although certain manufacturers offered special export models with larger-bore engines. On the other hand, certain American cars were made available with small-bore engine variants and some were offered with English coachbuilt bodywork, attracting many buyers.

Most British manufacturers could supply running chassis which the buyer could then have fitted with specialist coachwork. There were many firms, large and small, who could supply a large variety of open and closed bodies to the customer's choice.

This book, which follows the same pattern as its Olyslager Auto Library companion titles on American Cars of the 1930s, 1940s and 1950s, illustrates and briefly describes some 235 types of British cars produced from 1930 to 1934. Owing to the multiplicity of makes, models and types which were available during this period, it has proved impossible to show more than a random selection; this also necessitated a separate volume, entitled *British Cars of the Late Thirties—1935–1939*, to cover the second half of this eventful decade.

Piet Olyslager MSIA MSAE KIVI

1930

During the 1930 model year, ending in September, the British motor industry produced 236,528 motor vehicles, of which 169,669 were private cars and taxis. By September the total number of cars in use was 1,177,872, including 102,791 which were registered as 'hackneys' (a hackney carriage is 'a vehicle which stands or plies for hire in a street'—e.g. a taxi-cab). During the 1930 calendar year 155,707 new cars were registered in just under forty HP (horse-power rating) classes. The highest number was in the 8 HP class, namely 40,272. Next were 12 HP with 24,805, 15 HP with 22,282, 16 HP with 17,701, and 10 HP with 11,190. All the others contained well under ten thousand. A total of just under 30,000 vehicles was exported, namely 23,209 cars and 6,770 commercial vehicles. Their combined value was about £6·7 million. Car imports numbered 9,751, valued at just over £1·5 million.

4B Alvis Front-Wheel Drive

4A AC 16/56 Magna

4C Austin Seven

4A : **AC** (Acedes) Cars Ltd of Thames Ditton, Surrey, offered two chassis, namely the 16/40 Royal with 9 ft 5¼ in wheelbase and the 16/56 Magna with 9 ft 11¼ in wheelbase. Shown is an Aceca Coupé Cabriolet based on the latter. It cost £475 and like the 16/40 had a 1991-cc (65 × 100 mm) six-cylinder engine, rated at 15·7 HP. Tyres were 5.50-19.

4B : **Alvis** Straight-Eight 1½-Litre Supercharged Front-Wheel Drive racer, photographed at Brooklands about 1931. The driver was Thomas Dowling and the passenger was the car's owner, Ernie Coleman. In the 1930 TT the Alvis team swept their class in first, second and third position and only failed to beat the Alfa Romeo 1750s for

outright victory. The FA 8/15 eight-cylinder engine had a cubic capacity of 1491 cc (55 × 78·5 mm) and developed 95 bhp at 5500 rpm. It had an overhead camshaft, two magnetos and a multi-plate clutch with four-speed gearbox ahead of the engine.

4C : **Austin** Seven was first introduced in 1922 and continued until 1939 with periodic changes and improvements. Throughout this timespan, during which over ¼ million were sold, the engine remained basically the same : four-cylinder side-valve, 747·5-cc (56 × 76 mm), RAC rating 7·8 HP. The 1929/30 Saloon model shown is one of many survivors of this now legendary motor-car.

5A : **Austin** Seven Two-Seater sold at £130, including electric starting, lighting and horn, shock absorbers, air strangler, etc.

5B : **Austin** Seven Coupé had two seats and cost £140 (with sliding sunshine roof £5 extra). 'A dainty model that has made a very strong appeal to lady motorists', the sales catalogue claimed.

5C Austin Seven/Swallow

5A Austin Seven

5D Austin 16 HP

5B Austin Seven

5C : **Austin**/Swallow Saloon consisted of the standard Austin Seven chassis with special bodywork produced by the Swallow Side Car & Coach Building Co. of Blackpool (later Jaguar Cars of Coventry). Note V-shaped windscreen and slotted wheel stud holes. Swallow special coachwork was fitted also on other chassis, including Morris Cowley, Standard Big Nine, and Swift Ten.

5D : **Austin** 16 HP six-cylinder with new Open Road Five-Seater bodywork was offered at £325. Wheelbase was 9 ft 4 in, engine 2249-cc (65·5 × 111 mm) 36-bhp side-valve, rated at 15·9 HP.

1930

6A: **Austin** Twenty Ranelagh Enclosed Limousine was one of the Company's most expensive models, selling at £630 (£640 with sliding roof). Wheelbase was 11 ft 4 in. Chassis was also available with 10 ft 10 in wheelbase. Car was powered by a 3400-cc (79·5 × 114·5 mm) 49-bhp side-valve Six, rated at 23·5 HP.

6B: **Bentley** produced 4½- and 6½-Litre chassis. Shown is the famous 4½-Litre Supercharged model which had an OHC four-cylinder engine of 4398-cc capacity (100 × 140 mm). The supercharger, with twin SU carburettors, was fitted in front of the engine and radiator. Wheelbase was 10 ft 10 in, tyre size 6.00-21.

6C: **Ford** Models A and AF were assembled at the company's Trafford Park, Manchester, factory from 1928 until 1931, following tens of thousands of Model Ts. The Model A was virtually identical to the American parent car, differing mainly in having right-hand drive. The engine was a 3285-cc (98·4 × 108 mm) side-valve Four, rated at 24 HP. For those customers who wanted more economy, including lower HP tax rating, there was the 14·9 HP Model AF which had 77·6-mm bore but was otherwise similar. The AF had a cubic capacity of 2043 cc. Actual power output of the two engines was 40 bhp at 2200 rpm and 28 at 2600 respectively. Both cars had three-speed gearbox, 8 ft 7½ in wheelbase, 4.75-19 tyres on wire wheels and a transversal leaf spring for each axle. A 1930/31 Fordor Saloon model is shown.

6A Austin Twenty

6B Bentley 4½-Litre

6C Ford Model A(F)

7A: **Hillman** produced two types of cars, the 12·8 HP Fourteen and the 19·7 HP Straight 8. Various bodystyles were available and some are shown here at the Olympia Motor Show. The saloon in the centre is a Fourteen.

7B: **Hillman** Straight 8 Segrave Coupé was new for 1930 and was powered by a 2620-cc (63 × 105 mm) 52·5-bhp eight-cylinder in-line engine. Shown with the new car are Major Sir Henry Segrave, world land speed record holder, and Captain Irving, then Technical Director of the Hillman-Humber-Commer Combine (later known as Rootes Group).

7C: **Humber** Tourer was available on 16/50 and Snipe 10 ft wheelbase chassis, at £425 and £495 respectively. This specimen was photographed at the top of the St. Gotthard Pass in Switzerland in September, 1957.

7D: **Humber** top-line Pullman range was available with Limousine, Landaulette and Cabriolet De Ville bodywork. The latter sold at £1095, the other two at £775. The chassis was available at £495. Shown is a Pullman Landaulette, after having covered 170,000 miles. The 3·5-Litre six-cylinder engine developed 72 bhp and was rated at 23·8 HP.

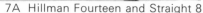
7A Hillman Fourteen and Straight 8

7B Hillman Straight 8

7C Humber 16/50

7D Humber Pullman

1930

PL 1138

8 Invicta 4½-Litre Standard

8 : **Invicta** 4½-Litre Standard Model had 100-bhp 29·1 HP six-cylinder OHV engine of 4467-cc cubic capacity (88·5 × 120·6 mm) with twin SU carburettors. Wheelbase was 10 ft 6 in. The Rudge-Whitworth wire wheels had 31 × 6 tyres. Standard chassis sold at £680, with saloon bodywork £795. Invicta Cars had their works at The Fairmile, Cobham, Surrey.

9A : **Invicta** 4½-Litre Sports Model was basically similar to the Standard Model (*q.v.*), modified mainly in respect of height. The chassis was upswept at the front and underslung at the rear, with a wheelbase of 9 ft 10 in. Radiator and dashboard were modified to suit. Other modifications included different springs, gear ratios, etc. Both cars were announced in late 1930, for the 1931 model year.

9B : **Jowett** supplied rugged little tourers, vans and other types, powered by a water-cooled horizontally-opposed twin-cylinder engine. This engine was in production for over 40 years, from 1910/11. Illustrated is one of a fleet of special four-seater Battery Staff Cars delivered to a York firm of military vehicle fleet hirers.

9C : **Lagonda** produced four-cylinder 14/60 and six-cylinder 16/65 and 3-Litre models. Illustrated is a surviving 3-Litre Special Tourer with fabric body and cycle wings.

9D : **Lea-Francis** 12/40 Type V with Weymann Sportsman's Coupé bodywork sold at £420 and sported two side-mounted spare wheels. Engine was a 1496-cc (69 × 100 mm) OHV Four, developing 38 bhp at 3800 rpm.

9A Invicta 4½-Litre Sports

9C Lagonda 3-Litre Special

9B Jowett 7 HP

9D Lea-Francis 12/40

1930

10A: **MG** 18/80 had an 80-bhp 2468-cc (69 × 110 mm) six-cylinder OHC engine with twin SU carburettors. It was designed entirely by MG, rather than based on a modified Morris chassis like the Company's smaller models. Some 750 18/80s were built with various open and closed body styles. Mk I models (from late 1928) had a three-speed gearbox, Mk II models (1929–32) had a four-speed gearbox, improved brakes, sturdier chassis, etc. Shown is a somewhat damaged Mk I Tourer.

10B: **Morgan** three-wheelers were available with 980-cc air-cooled and 1078- and 1096-cc water-cooled (shown) V-twin engines. All had 2-speed gearbox, shaft and chain final drive and 6-ft wheelbase. Prices ranged from £87 10s. to £145.

10C: **Morris** Minor was first made in 1929 with two-door Saloon and Tourer bodywork. From 1930 a 5-cwt van variant was available, an example of which is shown. The engine was an 847-cc (57 × 83 mm) OHC unit, with three-speed gearbox. The same basic engine was used in the contemporary MG M-type Midget.

10D: **Morris** Cowley was a popular rugged model with 1550-cc (69·5 × 102 mm) four-cylinder engine rated at 11·9 HP. The spiral bevel rear axle was driven through a multiplate clutch with cork insets and a three-speed gearbox. Tyres were 4.40-27 on steel spoke wheels. Wheelbase was 8 ft 9 in. The chassis cost £130, prices of complete cars ranged from £162 to £200. Shown is a Two-seater Tourer with dickey seat.

10B Morgan Super Sports Aero

10C Morris Minor

10A MG 18/80

10D Morris Cowley

11A Morris Isis Six

11B Rolls-Royce 20/25

11C Rolls-Royce Phantom II

11D Rolls-Royce Phantom II

11A: **Morris** Isis Six Sports Coupé was top-line model with 17·7 HP 2468-cc (69 × 110 mm) 6-cylinder OHC engine. Chassis price was £295, complete cars cost from £375 to £399. The wire wheels had 5.50-19 tyres. Wheelbase was 9 ft 6 in.

11B: **Rolls-Royce** 20/25 HP with Four-door Four-light Saloon bodywork by Arthur Mulliner Ltd. of Northampton. The 20/25 HP chassis had a wheelbase of 10 ft 9 in and was priced at £1185. Engine was a 3680-cc (82 × 114 mm) OHV Six, rated at 25·3 HP. Tyre size was 6.50-19. Note the side lights, incorporated in the forward end of the wings.

11C: **Rolls-Royce** Phantom II chassis with Belgian Van Den Plas bodywork. The Phantom II had 6.75-21 tyres and a 7668-cc (107·95 × 140 mm) six-cylinder OHV engine, rated at 43·3 HP.

11D: **Rolls-Royce** Phantom II chassis with 'Colonial' tourer-type bodywork. The chassis prices were £1850 (SWB) and £1950 (LWB).

12 Rolls-Royce Phantom II

13B Singer Junior

13C Singer Junior

13A Rover Light Six

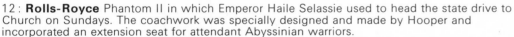

12 : **Rolls-Royce** Phantom II in which Emperor Haile Selassie used to head the state drive to Church on Sundays. The coachwork was specially designed and made by Hooper and incorporated an extension seat for attendant Abyssinian warriors.
13A : **Rover** Light Six Saloon had six-light Weymann body on 8 ft 10 in wheelbase chassis with 15.7 HP six-cylinder OHV engine. Gearbox was three-speed, tyre size 5.00-19. Other 1930 Rovers included 10/25, Two-Litre and Meteor models.
13B : **Singer** Junior Saloon, 500,000 miles after the owner bought it new for £160 in 1930 ('the garage threw in a free driving course that lasted a month ; not bad value for money', he recalled). The Junior had an 848-cc (56 × 86 mm) OHC four-cylinder engine of 7·78 HP and three-speed gearbox.
13C : **Singer** with a mascot. The St. Denys Sisters, well-known Music Hall artists, and their Singer Junior Sportsman's Coupé. This little 8 HP two-seater Coupé sold at £165 and was mechanically similar to the Junior Saloon except that the engine developed 19·6 bhp at 4000 rpm as compared with 16 at 3600.
13D : **Singer** Porlock Two-Seater on original run of 100 consecutive climbs of Porlock Hill, North Devon, which gave the model its name.

13D Singer Porlock

1930

14A : **Singer** Super Six Coupé was one of the company's top-line models and cost £350. The Saloon on the same 9 ft 6¾ in wheelbase chassis was sold at the same price. Engine was a 1920-cc (65·5 × 95 mm) 45-bhp OHV Six, rated at 15·91 HP. Singer also produced a smaller, 37-bhp 1792-cc side-valve Six, rated at 15·7 HP. This artist's impression in Rover's sales brochure did little credit to the car's actual appearance.

14B : **Standard** 9 HP chassis was available with several body types including the Teignmouth Fabric Saloon with sliding roof shown here. The basic saloon was known as Fulham (wb 8 ft 3 in and 7 ft 8 in resp.). Both had 4-cyl. 1287-cc side-valve engine. Standard also offered 6-cyl. 2054-cc 15 HP models.

14C : **Sunbeam** 25 HP was one of four types offered by this famous manufacturer. The six-cylinder OHV engine measured 80 × 120 mm (3619 cc) and developed 70 bhp. Treasury rating was 23·8 HP. The wheelbase was just over 11 ft 5 in, the tyre size 6.00-21. The Rally Weymann Saloon with side-mounted spare wheels cost £1075 and was supplied only to special order.

14B Standard 9 HP

14C Sunbeam 25 HP

14A   Singer Super Six

15A: **Triumph** offered a wide range of body styles on the 7 HP Model K chassis. Shown is a 1930/31 Open Two-seater which sold at £167.10s. It had an 832·24-cc (56·5 × 83 mm) 7·9 HP side-valve Four engine, developing 18 bhp. A Supercharged Sports Two-seater was offered also, priced at £250. Triumphs were among the earliest British cars to have hydraulic brakes.

15B: **Trojan** was available in Saloon and Tourer (shown) form and had many unconventional features including a valveless two-stroke four-cylinder engine located beneath the front seats, open epicyclic two-speed gearbox, chain drive to a solid rear axle (no differential), and long cantilever leaf springs, to list a few. It was produced with only minor changes from the early 1920s until 1930/31. After that it was continued only with van bodywork, notably for Brooke Bonds, until the Second World War. In 1930 Trojan Ltd. introduced a rear-engined car which was in small-scale production until 1936.

15C: **Vauxhall** introduced their new Cadet, with 2048-cc (67·5 × 95 mm) engine, rated at 16·9 HP. It supplemented the 2916-cc T and TL models. All had OHV Six engines. The Cadet had 8 ft 11 in wheelbase and 5.00-29 tyres on wire wheels.

15D: **Wolseley** Hornet was one of the first British cheap small six-cylinder engined cars. In a way it resembled the Morris Minor, with two extra 57 × 83 mm cylinders and bonnet to suit. Cubic capacity was 1271 cc, RAC rating 12·08 HP. Example shown has Hoyal Coupé coachwork.

15A Triumph 7 HP

15B Trojan Tourer

15C Vauxhall Cadet

15D Wolseley Hornet

1931

The September 1931 Census showed that the total number of motor vehicles in use in the United Kingdom was 1,560,349. This included 1,103,715 private cars and 89,182 'hackneys'. In the 1931 model year private car and taxi production totalled 158,997, a drop of over ten thousand compared with the previous year and obviously a result of the world-wide economic depression. Total production of all types of motor vehicles was 226,307, just over 10 per cent of which was exported. This also showed a decrease compared with the previous year. Imports amounted to 2,118 cars, valued at £467,785. The total number of new car registrations at home was 139,403 (excl. N. Ireland) with the largest number in the 8 HP class (36,354), followed by 12 HP (17,647), 10 HP (14,522), 16 HP (13,803), 14 HP (12,406) and 15 HP (12,164), the remaining HP classes all containing well under 10,000. In Northern Ireland 2,712 new cars were registered.

16B Alvis 16·95 HP Silver Eagle

16A AC 16/56

16C Alvis 20 HP Silver Eagle

16A : **AC** 16/56 four-door saloon. The 1991-cc OHC engine developed 56 bhp and drove the ¾-floating rear axle through a single dry-plate clutch, three-speed gearbox with right-hand gate change and 5·5 :1 worm type final drive.

16B : **Alvis** 16·95 HP Silver Eagle was first introduced in 1929 and continued into the thirties with detail improvements. Its six-cylinder engine had pushrod-operated overhead valves and a cubic capacity of 2148 cc (67·5 × 100 mm). Wheelbase was 10 ft 3 in and the 1931/32 four/five-seater Tourer version illustrated cost £595.

16C : **Alvis** 20 HP Silver Eagle was basically similar to the 16·95 HP but had 73-mm bore, resulting in 2511-cc cubic capacity. Two wheel-base lengths were available : 10 ft 3 in (Model TB) and 11 ft (Model TC chassis for Limousine body). Like the 16·95 HP it featured a Special Dual Ignition system, consisting of an aircraft type Polar Inductor Magneto, 'adapted by the use of special switches and high-tension coil to work as coil ignition for starting, or in the unlikely event of magneto failure'. The Mayfair Four-light Saloon shown sold at £775.

17A Armstrong Siddeley 12 HP

17B Aston-Martin 1½-Litre Sports

17C Austin Seven

17D Austin Sixteen

17A: **Armstrong Siddeley** offered six chassis, all with six-cylinder engine. They ranged from the 1434-cc 12 HP up to the 4960-cc 30 HP. Shown is a Six-Light Coach-Built Saloon on the 8 ft 9 in wheelbase 12 HP chassis which was available with either disc (shown) or wire spoke wheels.

17B: **Aston Martin** 1½-Litre Sports was powered by a 1496-cc (69·3 × 99 mm) twin-carburettor OHC engine and had 8 ft 6 in wheelbase. This is one of the team cars of the 1931 racing season, seen at the Montagu Motor Museum many years later. Its sister cars finished first and second in the 1931 Double-Twelve Race at the famous Brooklands track and won the Rudge Cup at Le Mans in 1932.

17C: **Austin** Seven 'Chummy' Tourer of 1930/31. These models had a shorter scuttle than before and a revised bonnet with two sets of louvres. In August 1931 the wheelbase was extended from 6 ft 3 in to 6 ft 9 in.

17D: **Austin** Sixteen chassis had a 2249-cc (65·6 × 111 mm) six-cylinder engine and 9 ft 4 in wheelbase. It cost £235. Complete cars, with factory-built bodywork, were in the £310 to £345 price range. Shown is a 1930-style Burnham four-door Saloon.

1931

18 Bentley 8-Litre

18 : **Bentley** 8-Litre had 7983-cc (110 × 140 mm) six-cylinder engine, rated at 44·9 HP. Shown is Forrest Lycett's 11-ft wheelbase racer. A 12-ft wheelbase chassis cost £1850. 4½- and 6½-Litre models, costing from £1050 to £1800 in chassis form, were available also. Model shown weighed 4725 lb, incl. driver, and maximum speeds at 4000 rpm in the indirect gears were 51, 72 and 96 mph respectively. Maximum speed in top gear was quoted as : 'Autobahn : 122 mph (still accelerating)'.

19B Crossley Six-Wheeler

19A   Bentley 8-Litre

19C Daimler Double Six

19A : **Bentley** 8-Litre chassis with Coupé bodywork. This was one of the last 'real Bentleys'. The Company was taken over by Rolls-Royce and re-organized as Bentley Motors (1931) Ltd., headquartered at Derby. New RR/Bentley models first made their appearance at the Olympia Motor Show in 1933. The May 1932 registration of the car shown gives some indication of the time it took for special coachwork to be hand-built.

19B : **Crossley** offered this six-wheeled saloon for 'colonial' use. It was powered by a six-cylinder 3·5-Litre engine, which drove both rear axles ('tandem drive'). Note the wire-spoke wheels and the fabric body. A similar model was offered by Morris-Commercial Cars Ltd. (*q.v.*).

19C : **Daimler** Double Six 50 was a huge car with either 12 ft 11½ in or 13 ft 7 in wheelbase. The 7136-cc (81·5 × 114 mm) V-12-cylinder engine was arranged in four blocks of three cylinders and had two carburettors. All Daimlers were supplied in chassis form only, no standard bodies were listed. The Double Six 50 chassis cost £1950. Shown is a surviving 1930/31 Sports model Corsica Drophead Coupé, one of only a few built. The Double Six name was revived in 1972 for the Daimler edition of the V12 Jaguar Saloon.

1931

20A: **Ford** Model A Fordor, beautifully restored and photographed forty years later. During the production span of the Model A (and Model AF and commercial vehicle derivatives; see also 1930) Ford built their new Dagenham plant. Production was transferred there in 1931, the last vehicle coming off the Trafford Park, Manchester, assembly line in October 1931. Just under 15,000 Model A and AF cars were built in the UK, following some 275,000 Model Ts (1911–28).

20B: **Hillman** range of 4-cyl. Fourteen and 8-cyl. Straight 8 and Vortic 8 models was supplemented in April, 1931, with a new 6-cyl. range named Wizard. It was available with 65-mm bore (15·7 HP) or 75-mm bore (20·9 HP) with no price difference, the latter intended especially for overseas markets.

20C: **Hillman** Wizard 75 with Coupé Cabriolet bodywork at the introduction of the new range in the Royal Albert Hall in London on 27 April, 1931.

20A Ford Model A

20B Hillman Wizard

20C Hillman Wizard

21A Hillman Wizard

21B Hillman Vortic

21C Hillman Minx

21A: **Hillman** Wizard was available with wire spoke or artillery wheels, the latter being fitted to this prototype car, shown during tests prior to its introduction. Artillery wheels had wooden spokes, secured between two metal plates at the centre. This construction method had long been used for gun carriages and limbers; hence the name.

21B: **Hillman** Vortic was produced during 1931–32 and had a 2618-cc (63 × 105 mm) eight-cylinder in-line OHV engine, developing 58 bhp at 3300 rpm and rated at 19·7 HP. The chassis cost £325 (£285 in 1932) and is shown with Cabriolet coachwork by Charlesworth Bodies Ltd. of Coventry.

21C: **Hillman** Minx prototype. When the first Minx was completed at Coventry William Rootes (the late Lord Rootes) himself took it abroad and tested it on the continent of Europe and in North Africa. He made it a practice to personally test each new model and is shown here (right, with the Minx on the Swiss-Italian border in May, 1931. The car made its public debut at the Olympia Motor Show in the following October and deliveries commenced, after a few modifications, in the Spring of 1932 (*q.v.*).

21D: **Humber** Snipe Tourers and Pullman Limousine photographed in Jamaica. Engine was 23·8 HP 3498·5-cc (80 × 116 mm) Six, wheelbase 10 ft and 11 ft respectively.

21D Humber Snipe and Pullman

1931

22A: **Humber** Pullman Limousine. In addition to the Snipe and Pullman models Humber offered the 16/50 which was similar to the Snipe but had a 15·7 HP 2110-cc (65 × 106 mm) engine like the Hillman Wizard. Tyre size was 6.00-20 for the Pullman, 5.50-19 for the 16/50 and Snipe.

22B: **Humber** Snipe Saloon demonstrating its off-road capabilities on Army grounds near Aldershot.

22C: **Humber** 16/50 Saloon, after not uncommon conversion, spending its old age as a breakdown tender. Note blackout masks on headlamps, a feature of World War II days.

22B Humber Snipe

22A Humber Pullman

22C Humber 16/50

23A: **Morris** Minor had 847-cc (57 × 83 mm) four-cylinder engine, rated at 8·05 HP. The chassis was available for £100, complete cars costing from £125 to £140. Wheelbase was 6 ft 6 in.

23B: **Morris** Oxford Six Tourer, still going strong after almost forty years and three owners. This model had a 30·5-bhp 1938-cc (63·5 × 102 mm) side-valve Six engine, rated at 14·9 HP. The chassis cost £185, complete cars from £250 to £285.

23C-D: **Morris-Commercial** Model 6D Saloon was built in limited numbers for 'colonial' and military use. The engine was a 26·8 HP six-cylinder with 85 × 125 mm bore and stroke, developing 74 bhp at 2800 rpm. Power was transmitted through a four-speed gearbox to the worm-drive tandem rear axles. There was also the Model TD which had a 17·9 HP four-cylinder engine with the same bore and stroke as the 6D. Basically a 6 × 4 truck chassis it was available with Tourer bodywork.

23A Morris Minor

23B Morris Oxford

23C Morris-Commercial 6D

23D Morris-Commercial 6D

1931

24A: **Riley** Nine had four-cylinder 1089-cc (60·3 x 95·2 mm) engine of 9·02 HP rating. The British Army used some which were slightly modified to meet their requirements for (limited) cross-country work. Tyre size, for example, was 5.25-21 instead of the standard 4.40-27. Most of the Army cars had four-door soft-top bodywork. A military saloon is shown.

24B: **Riley** Brooklands two-seater as produced during 1930-31 either in racing trim or road trim. It had basically the same 1089-cc engine as the Riley Nine but with pump cooling instead of thermo-syphon, electric fuel pump instead of gravity feed and other modifications. Wheelbase

was 8 ft (10 inches shorter than the Nine). Car shown was photographed during a rally at the remains of the old Brooklands race track on 11 June, 1967.

24C: **Rolls-Royce** Phantom II Sedanca de Ville with coachwork by Park Ward. The six-cylinder engine was of 7695-cc cubic capacity and rated at 43·3 HP. The chassis cost £1850 (short) or £1900 (long).

24D: **Rover** 2-Litre Coachbuilt Saloon was available in standard and more luxurious Regal trim. Both had 9 ft 3 in wheelbase and a 2023-cc six-cylinder power unit with four-speed gearbox. Shown is a 1930-style standard model.

24A Riley Nine

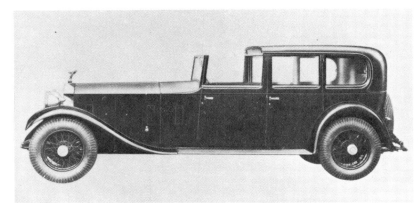

24C Rolls-Royce Phantom II

24B Riley Brooklands

24D Rover 2-Litre

25A Singer Junior

25B SS I

25C SS I

25A: **Singer** Junior Saloon was much the same as in 1930 but the three-speed gearbox was replaced by a four-speed unit. Wheelbase was 7 ft 6 in. The Saloon sold at £150, the Touring version at £135.

25B-C: **SS** stood for Swallow Sports, the name of the first motorcycle sidecars produced by the predecessors of Jaguar Cars Ltd. In 1931 SS became a *marque* in its own right, when the company introduced the SS I (for the 1932 model year). It was based on a Standard chassis, the engine of which was specially produced for Swallow. The SS I shown is still in daily use in Prague, Czechoslovakia.

25D: **Standard** Big Nine Special Tourer, priced at £195, had 1287-cc four-cylinder engine with four-speed gearbox and detachable wire wheels (basic Big Nine had three speeds and steel artillery wheels). Fabric Saloon variant cost £245.

25D Standard Big Nine

1931

26A: **Standard** Envoy Six had 2552-cc 20 HP engine with four-speed gearbox. Chassis cost £255, Weymann Saloon £385. Wheelbase was 9 ft 10 in.

26B: **Talbot** Ninety De Luxe Sports Tourer had a 17·9 HP 2276-cc (69·5 × 100 mm) OHV six-cylinder engine. Car was offered at £675, 'finished in black exterior material with red antique leather and red wire wheels'.

26C: **Trojan** Purley Fabric Saloon was one of the models which superseded the famous box-shaped Trojan cars of the 1920s. The four-cylinder engine was still of the two-stroke type with the cylinders arranged in pairs and each pair of pistons moving in unison, but it was now mounted at the rear. The earlier configuration with the engine mounted under the front seat was retained for the vans (see 1930).

26D: **Vauxhall** Cadet Coupé was based on Model VY 16·9 HP chassis (see also 1930). For export a 26·3 HP variant was introduced, designated model VX. For the VX the bore of the 6-cylinder engine was increased from 67·5 to 84·1 mm. With the stroke remaining at 95 mm this gave a piston displacement of 3177 cc. Brake horsepower was up from 42 to 47.

26A Standard Envoy Six

26C Trojan Purley

26B Talbot Ninety

26D Vauxhall Cadet

27A: **Vauxhall** Eighty 24 HP six-cylinder saloon, also known as Silent 80, was in production during 1931–32. It had a 3317-cc (80 × 110 mm) OHV engine, four-speed gearbox and 5.50-20 tyres.

27B: **Whitlock** cars are extremely rare and have never been numerous at the best of times. This rather derelict 20/70 specimen, registered in 1931, was discovered by Michael Sedgwick in 1963. During 1930–31 the 20/70 was supplied with a six-cylinder 3301-cc (76·2 × 120·7 mm) 72-bhp Meadows OHV engine, rated at 21·5 HP. Two chassis were available, Model A with 10 ft 4 in wheelbase at £650, Model B with 11 ft wheelbase at £700.

27C: **Wolseley** 21/60 cars were available with six-cylinder 2677-cc (75 × 101 mm) or eight-cylinder 2700-cc (65 × 101 mm) engine, both with overhead camshaft and rated at 20·93 and 21·01 HP respectively. Shown is a Model E7D 21/60 County Saloon which had 9 ft 6 in wheelbase and 5.50-18 tyres. The price was £445 (Chassis £295).

27D: **Wolseley** Hornet six-cylinder 7 ft 6½ in wheelbase chassis with Swallow two-seater coachwork.

27A Vauxhall Eighty

27C Wolseley 21/60

27B Whitlock 20/70

27D Wolseley Hornet/Swallow

1932

The 1932 model year saw a healthy increase in car production, amounting to almost 10% over the corresponding period ending September 1931. Private car and taxi output was 171,244 but a drop in commercial vehicle production kept the total production figure of all types down to 232,719. The year's export figure for cars rose to 31,797 units, the highest ever with the exception of 1929 when almost thirty-four thousand were shipped overseas. Sterling value of these two annual export figures, however, differed out of proportion at 3·93 million for 1932 and 5·47 million for 1929, suggesting an increase in overseas sales of smaller and cheaper cars. 2,762 foreign cars were imported. Home registrations from January to December amounted to 152,950 (excl. N. Ireland with just over 3000) with the 8 HP group still leading but rapidly losing ground to the 10 HPs. Exact figures were 34,068 and 24,623 respectively. Other HP classes in the over-10,000 league were 12 HP (23,581), 9 HP (18,154) and 14 HP (15,427). Only 187 cars were of a higher rating than 40 HP, compared with 303 in 1931 and 509 in 1930. In September the total number of vehicles in use was just over 1·6 million, including 1,149, 231 private cars and 86,743 'hackneys'.

28B Alvis 12/60

28A   AC 16/56 Magna

28C Aston Martin International

28A: **AC** 16/56 Magna had 56-bhp 1991-cc OHC engine, rated at 15·7 HP. A Sports version was available with a 60-bhp variant of the same power unit. The Coupé shown cost £400 and featured a dickey seat.

28B: **Alvis** TL 12/60 was available in chassis form at £395 or complete as two-seater Sports (£450) and Sports Saloon (shown, £495). The four-cylinder OHV engine was of 1645-cc (69 × 110 mm) capacity, rated at 11·8 HP. Power output was 52 bhp at 4000 rpm. The TJ 12/50

Alvis had basically the same engine but with 42-bhp output.

28C: **Aston Martin** International Four-Seater had a 1496-cc (69 × 99 mm) OHC four-cylinder engine, developing 56 bhp at 4500 rpm and rated at 11·9 HP. Transmission comprised four-speed gearbox and worm-drive rear axle.

29A : **Austin** supplied many Seven two-seaters to the British Army who used them for scouting and similar purposes. 1929–32 models had a WD-design box back body ; the front end sheet metal was like that of the contemporary civilian model. Initial equipment included 4.00-27 'knobbly' tyres. Shown is a 1931/32 model.

29B : **Austin** Ten-Four was a new addition to the Company's 1932 range. It was powered by an 1125-cc 9·99 HP side-valve four-cylinder engine which gave a top speed of over 56 mph. By April 1932, the full Austin range consisted of Seven, Ten-Four, Twelve-Six, 12, 16 and 20 HP models, with a wide variety of body styles.

29C-D : **Ford** of Britain had made American Model T and A cars (and commercial derivations TT and AA) for many years at their Manchester plant. In May 1932 the Model B (shown) was introduced. This car was produced in the new Dagenham plant in three basic versions : Model B (4-cyl., 24 HP, until Oct. 1934), Model BF (small-bore 4-cyl., 14·9 HP, until 1935) and Model 18 (V-8-cyl., 30 HP, until Sept. 1933).

29C Ford Model B

29A Austin Seven

29B Austin Ten-Four

29D Ford Model B

1932

30A : **Ford** opened their new Dagenham factory in 1931 and the first all-British Ford car to emerge was the 8 HP Model Y. It was, in appearance, a scaled-down replica of the American Model B. It was powered by a 933-cc (56·6 × 92·5 mm) side-valve four-cylinder engine. Drive to the 5·42:1 spiral-bevel rear axle was transmitted via a single dry plate clutch and a three-speed gearbox with synchromesh. Wheelbase was 7 ft 6 in, track 3 ft 8 in. Early production had 4.00-18 tyres. Suspension was the same as on all contemporary Ford cars, using transverse semi-elliptic leaf springs.

30B-C : **Ford** 8 HP was restyled in the summer of 1932. The new 'Popular Ford' (later to be named Ford Popular) was again a small-scale version of the American Ford, this time the 1933 Model 40 (which was not marketed in the UK until about a year later). Within the Ford organization the 8 HP Model Y was known also as Model 19E.

30B Ford 8 HP Model Y

30A Ford 8 HP Model Y

30C Ford 8 HP Model Y

31A Frazer-Nash TT Replica

31A: **Frazer-Nash** TT Replica model was powered by a 1496-cc (69 × 100 mm) OHV four-cylinder engine with twin SU carburettors, rated at 11·9 HP. Engine performance was 'according to owner's requirements'. Suspension was by quarter-elliptic leaf springs and wheelbase was 8 ft 6 in. Several other models were offered by the manufacturers, AFN Ltd. of Isleworth, Middlesex.

31B: **Hillman** sold their first Minx cars in early 1932 and they were an immediate success. The engine was a 9·8 HP 1185-cc (63 × 95 mm) side-valve Four, developing 25 bhp at 3600 rpm. Gearbox was three-speed, wheelbase 7 ft 8 in. The chassis cost £120 and there were four Saloon and two Tourer body types available from the factory (price range £159 to £198).

31C: **Hillman** Minx; an early model still going strong forty years later. This beautifully preserved car belongs to Mr. Paul Gallifant of the Colchester Vintage Motor Club.

31C Hillman Minx

31B Hillman Minx

1932

32 Hillman Minx

32 : **Hillman** Minx Tourer was driven by Captain T. Yates Benyon from London to Calcutta in 1932 in an attempt to beat the mail boat. He covered 6,803 miles in 33 days.

33A : **Hillman** Minx with attractive two-seater bodywork by Carbodies of Coventry. The price was £185 and for only just over £2 10s. extra one could have the radiator stone guard (shown) and a spare wheel cover.

33B : **Hillman** Wizard, introduced in 1931 (*q.v.*), seen here on the desert sands near Cheops, Egypt, with Pyramid in the background.

33C : **Humber** Snipe Saloon had 23·8 HP 3·5-litre six-cylinder engine and four-speed gearbox. The 16/50 model was similar except for 15·7 HP 2·1-litre engine. The wire wheels had 5.50-19 tyres. Car shown succesfully completed a journey across the Andes.

33B Hillman Wizard

33A Hillman Minx

33C Humber Snipe

1932

34A: **Humber** Pullman Limousine had same engine as the Snipe but had 11 vs. 10 ft wheelbase and 6.00-20 vs. 5.50-19 tyres. The car shown was supplied to the Dunlop Rubber Company for tyre testing purposes. When the picture was taken, in March 1934, the car had covered 100,000 miles, working out at 300 miles per day five days a week.

34B: **Invicta** offered three chassis, the 12 HP, the 30 HP and the 30 HP Sports, at £335, £680 and £750 respectively. Illustrated is a £425 Five-seater Saloon on the 12 HP chassis, which was known as the Small Invicta. It had a six-cylinder OHC engine of 1498-cc capacity (57 × 97·9 mm), developing 45 bhp at 4400 rpm.

34C: **Invicta** 4½-Litre 30 HP Sports Open Four-Seater cost £875. It had a six-cylinder OHV engine of 4467-cc (88·5 × 120 mm) capacity, developing 108 bhp at 3200 rpm. Like the Small Invicta (q.v.) it had a dropped frame, underslung at the rear, with 9 ft 10 in wheelbase. The basic 4½-Litre, available with Saloon bodywork at £795, had 10 ft 6 in wheelbase.

34B Invicta 12 HP

34A Humber Pullman

34C Invicta 4½-Litre

35A Lagonda Two-Litre

35B Lagonda Three-Litre

35C Lea-Francis 1½-Litre

35A : **Lagonda** Two-Litre Speed Weymann Fabric Saloon was available in black, maroon and green at £695. Any deviation from these colourings cost £10 extra. Other extra-cost options included cycle type wings, £10, and semi-panelled Bodywork in place of fabric, £25. The two-litre (1954·32-cc) engine had twin overhead camshafts, interchangeable inlet and exhaust valves and hemispherical combustion chambers, machined all over. Gearbox was four-speed, wheelbase 10 ft, tyre size 5.00-31. The two-litre models were also available in supercharged form, boosting the power output from 67 to 90 bhp, both at 4200 rpm.

35B : **Lagonda** produced two-litre four-cylinder and three-litre six-cylinder models. Illustrated here is a Three-Litre Selector Special Panelled Weymann Saloon, priced at £1065. A luggage boot for two suitcases was fitted at the rear. The car had a 3181-cc (75 × 120 mm) OHV engine and a special 'Selector' vacuum-operated gearbox, manufactured under Maybach licence. It provided two ranges of four forward speeds, controlled from the top of the steering column. A conventional gear lever was used for reverse and for selecting high and low ratio.

35C : **Lea-Francis** 1½-Litre Hyper-Sports Four-seater Tourer was one of several models offered with super-charged engine. The 1496-cc (69 × 100 mm) OHV four-cylinder engine developed 72 bhp and was rated at 11·9 HP. The Cozette blower (super-charger) was driven at engine speed by bevel gears direct from the crankshaft. Gearbox was four-speed, wheelbase 9 ft 3 in. Price of Tourer shown and Two-Seater model was £550. Fabric Saloon version cost £650.

35D : **Lea-Francis** 16/70 HP De Luxe Coachbuilt Saloon. This model sold for £495 (£505 with sliding roof) and had a 50-bhp 1991-cc (65 × 100 mm) OHC six-cylinder power unit, rated at 15·7 HP. Lea-Francis 2-Litre models were generally similar but had 9 ft 3 in vs. 9 ft 6 in wheelbase, single spare wheel and other detail differences.

35D Lea-Francis 16/70

1932

36A: **MG** cars of various types in dealer's showroom. In background, left to right: 18/80 Mark II Speed Model (£630), Two-seater (£625), and Saloon (£670). In the centre is an 8/33 Midget M-type Panelled Two-seater (£185), behind a Midget C-type Montlhery. The latter was a competition model, developed from the M-type. It had a two-seater racing body with cowled radiator and was priced at £490 (with supercharger £575).

36B: **MG** Magna F-type was produced during 1931–32 and had a six-cylinder engine developed from the Midget M-type. It was a 1271-cc OHC unit with an output of 37·2 bhp at 4100 rpm. Some 1250 were built, with three bodystyles. Shown is a four-seater Tourer, Model F3, with non-original headlamps and bonnet strap.

36C: **Morris** Minor now had a side-valve engine, replacing the earlier overhead-cam unit but bore and stroke were the same (57 × 83 mm, 847 cc). Several open and closed body styles were available, including this 5-cwt light van.

36B MG Magna F-type

36A MG

36C Morris Minor

37A-B: **Morris** Cowley was available with 1550-cc (69·5 × 102 mm) engine, rated at 11·9 HP or with 1802-cc (75 × 102 mm) engine, rated at 13·9 HP. The latter was known also as the 14/32. The 'ghost view' clearly shows the general layout of the car. Note pipe between top of engine and carburettor: the air cleaner was in the dummy valve rocker cover. Transmission was three-speed, wheelbase 8 ft 9 in, tyre size 5.00-19.

37C: **Morris** Isis Six was top-line model with 2468-cc (69 × 110 mm) six-cylinder OHV engine rated at 17·7 HP. The chassis was available at £250, the complete car cost £100 more. The wheelbase was 10 ft, the transmission four-speed and the tyre size 5.50-19.

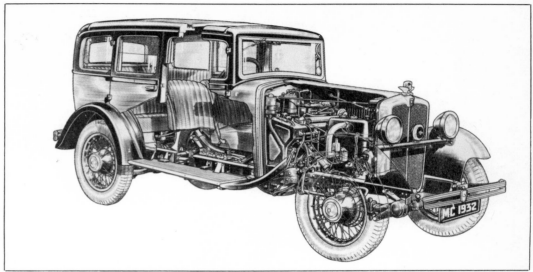

37B Morris Cowley

37A Morris Cowley

37C Morris Isis Six

1932

38A: **Morris** display at Guildford Distributors. On the left are the Sixes, on the right is a selection of Cowleys, with an Oxford Six at the far end. In the centre is an MG Midget.
38B: **Riley** Alpine five-seater Four-Light Saloon was introduced in late 1931 and continued until 1934. It had a 49-bhp 1633-cc (60·3 × 95·2 mm) six-cylinder OHV engine, rated at 14 HP.
38C: **Rolls-Royce** 40/50 HP Phantom II chassis with Coupé bodywork, photographed in 1972. The 7768-cc OHV six-cylinder engine was rated at 43·3 HP. The 20/25 HP model also had six cylinders but was of less than half this cubic capacity and rated at 25·3 HP. Both had four-speed gearbox and servo brakes.

38A Morris

38B Riley Alpine

38C Rolls-Royce 40/50

39A: **Rover** 10/25 Weymann Sportsman's Coupé with built-in rear luggage locker sold at £185 (sliding roof £5 extra). Saloon bodywork was available at slightly higher price. Engine was 1185-cc (63 × 95 mm) four-cylinder, rated at 9·8 HP, with three-speed gearbox. Rear axle drive was by worm. Wheelbase 8 ft 8 in.

39B: **Rover** Pilot was a 12 HP six-cylinder car available as coach-built or Weymann Saloon, or as Weymann Sportsman's Coupé. All three were priced the same at £245. The chassis cost £165. The 1410-cc OHV engine developed 30 bhp at 3600 rpm.

39C: **Singer** produced a wide range of models, varying from the £130 Junior Two-Seater to the £480 Kaye Don Six Saloon. Illustrated here is a Nine Sports Coupé which took part in the Monte Carlo Rally. It had a 972-cc (60 × 86 mm) 24·9-bhp OHC four-cylinder engine, rated at 8·93 HP. It was introduced in August, 1932, for the 1933 model year.

39D: **Standard** Little Nine Two-seater was smallest and cheapest (£145) of Standard's range which comprised Little and Big Nine, Sixteen and Twenty models. The little Nine had a 22-bhp 1005-cc (60·25 × 88 mm) side-valve Four engine. The Sixteen and Twenty were Sixes.

39B Rover Pilot

39C Singer Nine

39D Standard Little Nine

39A Rover 10/25

1932

40A : **Standard** Little Nine Special Saloon was priced at £169. The Basic Saloon, which had less luxurious specification and no bumpers, cost £155. Both had 7 ft 6 in wheelbase.

40B : **Standard** Big Nine range comprised Tourers and Saloons, costing from £195 up to £255. Shown is the £255 Special Saloon. All had 1287-cc 26-bhp four-cylinder side-valve engine and four-speed gearbox.

40C : **Talbot** 14/45 HP Light Six Scout was available with two- or four-door Saloon body-work, both at £395. The engine was a 1666-cc (61 × 95 mm) OHV Six with an output of 45 bhp at 4500 rpm, rated at 13·8 HP.

40D : **Talbot** Seventy-Five Two/Three-Seater with double dickey seat was one of 11 body options on this 17·9 HP £425 chassis with 9 ft 6 in wheelbase. Engine was an OHV six-cylinder of 2276-cc capacity (69·5 × 100 mm). Prices of complete cars ranged from £525 (model shown) to £695 (Limousine and Landaulette).

40B Standard Big Nine

40C Talbot 14/45

40D Talbot Seventy-Five

40A Standard Little Nine Special

41A Talbot Ninety

41B Triumph Super Seven

41D Wolseley Hornet Special/Swallow

41C Vauxhall Cadet

41A: **Talbot** Ninety De Luxe Sports Saloons had same engine and wheelbase as Seventy-Five models but a 10 ft wheelbase chassis was also available in this series. Model shown was priced at £695.

41B: **Triumph** Super Seven Four-door Pillarless Saloon Mark II was an attractive small car with an 832-cc side-valve four-cylinder engine, developing 19·8 bhp at 3500 rpm and rated at 7·9 HP. Tyre size was 4.00-27, wheelbase 6 ft 9 in. It had a rear-mounted fuel tank with vacuum feed (front-mounted with gravity feed on Mark I).

41C: **Vauxhall** Cadet was a popular car, selling at £280 in 16·9 HP Saloon form. It had a 2048-cc 42-bhp engine. Other 1932 Vauxhall offerings were the Eighty and Eighty L (LWB) with 3317-cc power unit. All engines were OHV Sixes. The Cadet was available for export with a 3177-cc 47-bhp engine and was the first major 'fruit' of the take-over of Vauxhall Motors by the General Motors Corporation.

41D: **Wolseley** Hornet Special chassis with Swallow open four-seater bodywork. Compared with the standard model, the Hornet Special offered extra-performance features such as twin carburettors and oil cooler. Other 1932 Wolseleys were 16/60 and 21/60 OHC Sixes; the Eight was no longer available.

1933

Production, registration and export figures were all going upward. Model year production figures showed 220,779 cars, including taxis and 65,508 commercial vehicles, including buses. Calendar year exports amounted to a total of 41,028 cars, representing a value of over £5 million. New car registrations from January to December were now led by the 10 HP class with 48,938 units, closely followed by 44,484 8 HPs. 12 HPs came third with 28,909 registrations, fourth and fifth were the 9 HPs with 13,319 and the 14 HPs with 12,149 units. In the 16 HP class just over nine thousand new cars were registered and the remaining classes were way behind. In Northern Ireland there were 3,484 new car registrations. Total new vehicle registrations numbered just under 290,000, of which 186,543 were cars and 4,068 'hackneys'.

September census figures revealed that there were some 1·7 million motor vehicles in use in the United Kingdom. This included almost one and a quarter million private cars. The number of 'hackneys' remained steady at 86,805. During 1933 slightly more than 4,000 motor vehicles were imported, the majority being cars (complete and in chassis form), namely 3,619 units.

42B Alvis Speed 20

42A AC Ace 16/56

42A : **AC** Ace 16/56 Tourer or Drophead Coupé had 9 ft 4 in wheelbase and the familiar 2-litre (1991-cc) four-cylinder OHC engine which in this application developed 56 bhp at 3500 rpm. The car had seating for four and cost £395.

42B : **Alvis** Speed 20 with Cross and Ellis Tourer coachwork. The Speed 20 was first introduced in 1932 and with 90 mph from 2½ litres was a sensation at the time. The SB model shown, introduced in September 1933, differed from the original SA design in having independent front suspension and all-synchromesh gearbox. The six-cylinder OHV engine developed 95 bhp at 4000 rpm. The Speed 20 was produced until 1936, when it became the Speed 25 with 3½-litre engine.

43A: **Armstrong Siddeley** Saloon on 15 HP Long chassis. This chassis had a 13 ft 9 in wheelbase, compared with 12 ft 10 in for the normal 15 HP. Both types had 2169-cc side-valve engine, self-changing four-speed gearbox and permanent jacks.

43B: **Aston-Martin** 12/50 Saloon had a 1493-cc (69 × 99 mm) OHV four-cylinder 55-bhp engine, rated at 11·9 HP. Gearbox was four-speed and the chassis had a wheelbase of 9 ft 10 in and a track of 4 ft 4 in. Luxuriously equipped, the complete car cost £595.

43C: **Aston-Martin** 12/70 Le Mans Two-seater sold at the same price as the Saloon, £595. The chassis was generally similar, with the main exceptions of a different cylinder head design, resulting in 70 bhp at 4750 rpm and 1 ft 4 in shorter wheelbase. Final drive ratio was 4·66:1 compared with 5·1:1 on the Saloon. Both had 5.25-18 tyres and 4 ft 4 in track.

43D: **Austin** Ten-Four, powered by a 21-bhp 1125-cc (63·5 × 86 mm) side-valve Four engine, rated at 9·9 HP, was available with four body styles, priced from £148 to £168. This preserved Saloon model is owned by Mr. De La Mare of St. Helier, Jersey, C.I.

43A Armstrong Siddeley 15 HP

43B Aston-Martin 12/50

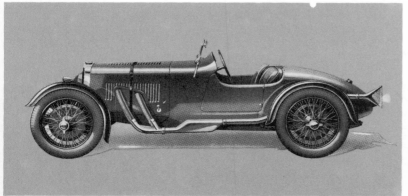

43C Aston-Martin 12/70

43D Austin Ten-Four

1933

44A Austin Light Twelve-Six

44C Bedford VYX Provincial Taxi

44B Austin Twenty

44A : **Austin** Light Twelve-Six was similar to the Austin Twelve-Four. Both had 8 ft 10 in wheelbase and 4.75-19 tyres but engine capacity was 1496-cc (61·25 × 84·63 mm) for the Six and 1535-cc (69·3 × 101·6 mm) for the Four. Power output was the same, namely 24 bhp at 2400 rpm, but HP rating was 13·9 and 11·9 HP respectively. Saloon De Luxe prices were £218 and £198 respectively.

44B : **Austin** Twenty had 11 ft 4 in wheelbase chassis with side-valve Six engine of 3400-cc (79·5 × 114·5 mm) capacity, rated at 23·4 HP. The chassis cost £350 and could be supplied with Limousine (shown) or Landaulette body-work in a price range from £498 up to £575. Other contemporary Austin Sixes were the 1·5-Litre Light Twelve (q.v.) and the 2·2-Litre Sixteen.

44C : **Bedford** Provincial Taxi was produced by Messrs. Doran, Taggart & Co., on Model VYX 12-cwt commercial (van) chassis. It was designed specifically for provincial town and country use. The VYX chassis had the same 16·9 HP engine as the Vauxhall Cadet car but for export it was available with 26·3 HP engine (Model VXC).

45A Daimler 15 HP

45B Daimler 25 HP

45C Ford Model BF.

45A: **Daimler** 15 HP with Coupé bodywork. The 15 HP was new and the only Daimler model with poppet valves (OHV) rather than sleeve valves. The bore and stroke were 63·5 × 95 mm, resulting in 1805-cc cubic capacity. Power output was 42·5 bhp at 3600 rpm.

45B: **Daimler** 25 HP had 3568-cc sleeve-valve engine, producing 61 bhp at 3200 rpm. Wheelbase was just over 11 ft 10 in, tyre size 6.00-20. This Saloon sold at £950.

45C: **Ford** Model B with 24 HP four-cylinder engine (3285-cc, 98·425 × 107·95 mm) and Model BF with 14·9 HP engine (as B but 77·6-mm bore, 2043-cc) were produced in Britain during 1932–35. They were originally similar to the 1932 US Ford Model B and Model 18 (same car with V8 engine; produced in Britain as C18R, 1932–33) but when the US Ford Motor Co. replaced these models by the modernized 1933 Model 40, the British Dagenham plant continued the Model B body shell with the four-cylinder 14·9 and 24 HP engine. These later models differed from the original in having 'skirted' front wings with streamlined side lights, different bumpers and a straight, rather than curved, headlamp tie bar as exemplified by this 1933/34 model BF Saloon. Wheelbase was 8 ft 10 in, tyre size 5.25-18, price £225. The models B and BF were also known as the AB and ABF and their chassis serial number prefixes consisted of these designations. The surviving example shown has some non-original features.

45D: **Ford** 8 HP Model Y underwent some further styling changes. The radiator grille was deeper ('long-rad' model; earlier models now known as 'short-rad') and the matching bumper had a curved-down centre section. Body style availability now included this four-door model. Originally the 8 HP two- and four-door saloons were named Tudor and Fordor respectively, following the American Ford custom. Later the more British sounding terms Single- and Double-entrance Saloon were used.

45D Ford Model Y

1933

46A: **Ford** Model Y Tudor sold at £120 but for an extra £13 the well-known firm of Jennings & Sons in Sandbach supplied a three-door utility car conversion as shown here. The Model Y was available also in chassis form, at £97 10s, for mounting special bodywork. Jennings did a similar conversion on the Ford Model BF for £14 10s.

46B: **Ford** 5-cwt Van was unveiled at a Ford Motor Co. exhibition at the White City, London, in October 1932. Mechanically it resembled the Model Y car. The loading capacity was 50 cu. ft and the rear door opening measured 3 ft 6½ in wide by 3 ft 0½ in high. The complete vehicle was priced at £115. At the same time a 12-cwt 86 cu. ft van was introduced on the Model B chassis, at £168. Normally fitted with the 24 HP Four engine, it could also be ordered with the 14·9 HP variant.

46A Ford Model Y

46B Ford Model Y

47A: **Frazer-Nash** produced Short and Long chassis with TT Replica (shown) and Colmore body styles. Both had a 1½-litre four-cylinder engine with magneto or coil ignition. The solid rear axle was chain-driven.

47B: **Hillman** Minx, introduced a year earlier, soon made a name for itself and became the company's main line. In addition to the chassis at £120, four Saloon models were available ranging from £159 to £195, as well as a two- and a four-door Tourer, at £175 and £159 respectively. One of the latter is shown, with 5.50-18 tyres replacing the standard 4.50-18 size. Wheelbase was 7 ft 8 in, as before.

47A Frazer-Nash 1½-Litre TT Replica

47B Hillman Minx

1933

48A Hillman Minx

48A: **Hillman** Minx Saloon car used by the Amsterdam Police for instructional purposes.
48B: **Hillman** Minx chassis was available at £120 for the mounting of specialist coachwork as exemplified by this Convertible Coupé.
48C: **Hillman** Aero Minx was available in Chassis, Sports Saloon and March Special Tourer variants. Shown is the Sports Saloon, which was priced at £245. Mechanically they were similar to the standard Minx except that the chassis was 'underslung' and had a wheelbase of 7 ft 4 in.

48B Hillman Minx

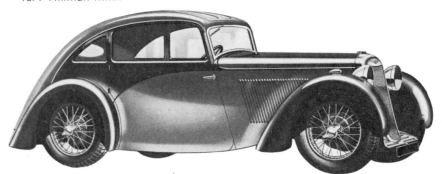

48C Hillman Aero Minx

49A : **Hillman** Wizard Saloon, priced at £285 whether fitted with 2110-cc or optional 2810-cc engine, was in its last year. Shown is a works car with caravan on their way from Coventry to the Cairo Motor Show by road in January, 1933.

49B : **Humber** Twelve shown negotiating a hill in Yorkshire. This car, which sold at £265 in Saloon form, had a 44-bhp 1669-cc (69·5 × 110 mm) side-valve power unit, rated at 11·98 HP, and an 8 ft 2¼ in wheelbase. Gearbox was four-speed.

49C-D : **Humber** Pullman chassis were supplied with Limousine, Landaulette, Limousine De Ville and Sedanca De Ville coachwork at prices ranging from £735 to £895. The bare chassis cost £425. They were mechanically similar to the Humber Snipe, with 23·8 HP 3·5-litre 76-bhp engine, but wheelbase was 9½ in longer, at 11 ft. Cars shown were delivered by The Car Mart Ltd. in January, 1933, for use by the Duke and Duchess of York. The coachwork was by Humber Ltd.

49B Humber Twelve

49C Humber Pullman

49A Hillman Wizard

49D Humber Pullman

50A Humber Snipe

50A: **Humber** Snipe 80 chassis with Ambulance bodywork leading a convoy of Hillman cars which formed part of the Empire Day celebrations in Brisbane, Australia. The Snipe chassis was available for the mounting of special bodywork and cost £345.

50B: **Jowett** offered Type 3G Short and Long models, each with various body styles. Illustrated is a standard Long Coachbuilt Saloon. Jowetts featured a water-cooled low-tax twin-cylinder engine of the horizontally-opposed type but provided passenger accommodation equal to many much larger cars.

50B Jowett 3G Long

51A Lagonda 3-Litre

51A: **Lagonda** offered a relatively wide range of chassis and complete cars. Shown is a 3-Litre 21 HP chassis with factory-supplied Weymann Sports Saloon bodywork, which cost £1065 in May, 1933 (chassis price £827). This fine specimen was completely restored and belongs to Mr. C. H. Sherwood of Worcestershire. The 3181-cc OHV Six engine produces 78 bhp at 3800 rpm.

51B: **Lanchester** produced two models, the four-cylinder 10 HP and the six-cylinder 18 HP. The latter had a 2504-cc (69·5 × 110 mm) 57-bhp OHV engine, 9 ft 7 in wheelbase and 5.25-18 tyres. The 10 HP and 18 HP both featured Daimler Fluid Flywheel with self-changing gearbox.

51C: **MG** Magna L-type was developed from the 1931–32 Magna F-type. Engine was 41-bhp six-cylinder 1086-cc OHC unit with twin SU carburettors. Gearbox was four-speed. Some 575 were built during 1933–34, with open two- and four-seater, four-seater Salonette and two-seater Coupé bodywork. A two-seater is shown.

51B Lanchester 18 HP

51C MG Magna

52A MG Magnette

52B MG Magnette

52C: **Morgan** offered four models, all with V-twin 1100-cc (85·7 × 95 mm) 9·1 HP engine, three-speed gearbox, worm and chain final drive, 6ft wheelbase and 18 × 3 Dunlop Magna wheels. Although the cylinder dimensions were the same, the engines were side- or overhead-valve, and air- or water-cooled. Shown is a water-cooled side-valve model.

52D: **Morris** Minor was supplied in some numbers to the British Army with special signals bodywork not unlike that mounted on the WD Austin Seven. The Minor, which was in production during 1929–34 with periodical improvements, had an 847-cc (57 × 83 mm) engine, rated at 8 HP. Picture shows car in use as radio link vehicle with artillery unit.

52C Morgan Three-Wheeler

52A: **MG** Magnette K1 pillarless Saloon had Wilson patent pre-selector self-changing gearbox and was also available in chassis and tourer form. The K2 had a conventional gearbox and sold in chassis form and as a two-seater. The K1 had 9 ft wheelbase, K2 and K3 (*q.v.*) 7 ft 10 in.
52B: **MG** K3 was racing version of the Magnette K-series (winner of 1933 Ulster TT). It had a two-seater racing body with flat tail and slab tank. 1934 models had a pointed tail section. During 1933–34 a total of 32 was produced. Engine was a supercharged 1086-cc (57 × 71 mm) OHC six-cylinder, developing 120 bhp at 6500 rpm. Gearbox was four-speed pre-selector type.

52D Morris Minor

53A Morris Minor

53B Morris Ten-Four

53C : **Morris** Six cars, such as the Oxford and Isis, together with numerous other medium and large size cars, were in many instances converted into ambulances when war broke out in 1939. This 'War Emergency Ambulance' was built on a reconditioned Morris chassis by P. G. Page Ltd., Motor Engineers of Colchester, Essex.
53D : **Riley** Nine Monaco Saloon. This 9 HP model was in production during 1930—37 with periodical improvements and modifications. The four-cylinder pushrod OHV engine developed 27 bhp (later 29) and was of 1089-cc capacity.

53C Morris Six

53D Riley 9 HP Monaco

53A : **Morris** Minor 5-cwt van was very popular with butchers, grocers and other foodstuff traders. Body style shown was strictly 1934.
53B : **Morris** Ten-Four was introduced in 1933 and was available with Saloon, Tourer (shown) and Special Coupé bodywork. The engine was a 1292-cc (63·5 × 102 mm) side-valve unit of 10 HP RAC rating. The four-speed gearbox had synchromesh on third and top gear. Wheelbase was 8 ft, tyre size 4.50-19. This model was continued through 1934 and sold at £169 10s.

54A: **Rover** Family Ten Coachbuilt Saloon cost £195 with three-speed gearbox. The 1185-cc (63 × 95 mm) four-cylinder OHV engine developed 25 bhp at 3600 rpm and for an extra £5 the customer could order optional four-speed transmission. Wheelbase was 8 ft 8 in, tyre size 4.50-18.

54B: **Rover** Ten Special was offered with two standard bodies, the Coachbuilt Saloon (shown) at £228 and the Coachbuilt Coupé at £248. A choice of special bodies was available also. The car featured Protectoglass windscreen, Startix automatic restarter (a system whereby the starter automatically re-engaged if the engine stalled), sliding roof, folding luggage grid, etc. Engine was same as in Family Ten (*q.v.*) but output was 27 bhp at 3800 rpm and four-speed gearbox with freewheel was standard.

54C: **Singer** offered Nine, Twelve, Fourteen, Two-Litre and Silent Six models in a price range of £159 up to £365. Shown is a Nine Four-seater Sports costing £185. Power unit was an OHC Four of 972-cc cubic capacity (60 × 86 mm). Gearbox was four-speed, wheelbase 7 ft 8 in. Note the fine array of trophies won by this car.

54D: **Singer** Nine Sports Coupé was an attractive little car, priced at £199. Standard models had a 24·5-bhp (later 26·5) engine but the Four-seater Sports and the Sports Coupé were powered by a 28-bhp (later 31) variant. Treasury rating of both engines was 8·93 HP.

54A Rover Family Ten

54B Rover Ten Special

54C Singer Nine

54D Singer Nine

55A: **SS** Cars Ltd. offered two models, the six-cylinder SS I based on Standard Sixteen mechanical components and the SS II which used the Standard Little Nine as a basis. The SS I, which is illustrated here, differed from the 1931–32 model mainly in having restyled wings and more elegant bodystyling. The SS II could be called a scaled-down version of the SS I.

55B: **Standard** introduced their successful Big and Little Nine models in 1932. Shown is the 1933 edition of the Little Nine De Luxe Saloon. It differed from the original model mainly in having 'skirted' front wings and a more rounded roofline. Basic models had painted headlamps and no bumpers. Engine was a 1006-cc (60·25 × 88 mm) 8·9 HP Four.

55C: **Sunbeam** Speed Model Coachbuilt Close-Coupled Saloon was priced at £745. The chassis was available at £500. Power unit was a 20·9 HP OHV Four of 2916-cc cubic capacity (75 × 110 mm). Wheelbase was 10 ft, tyre size 5.25-20. It was designed to give a high cruising speed and could be driven 'with the same ease and comfort as an ordinary touring car'.

55D: **Sunbeam** 16 HP Six-Cylinder Four-Seater Coupé, costing £695, had a 2193·6-cc (70 × 95 mm) OHV engine, with 18·2 HP treasury rating. Gearbox was four-speed synchromesh twin-top, wheelbase 10 ft 6¼ in, tyre size 30 × 5.25. The car had controlled shock absorbers and a central method of chassis lubrication.

55B Standard Little Nine

55C Sunbeam Speed Model

55A SS I

55D Sunbeam 16 HP

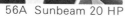
56A Sunbeam 20 HP

56D Vauxhall Light Six

56B Talbot 105

56C Triumph Southern Cross

56A: **Sunbeam** 20 HP Coachbuilt Saloon cost £795 and was most expensive of the range with the exception of the Limousine on the same chassis which had an ex-works price tag of £895. The 20 HP models (actual rating 23·8 HP) had a 3317·5-cc (80 × 110 mm) OHV Six engine.

56B: **Talbot** offered five chassis types, including the 105, which was available only in chassis form (£525). Shown is a 105 with coachbuilt two-door Saloon bodywork. The engine was a 2970-cc (75 × 112 mm) OHV Six, rated at 20·9 HP but actually developing 100 bhp at 4500 rpm. All Talbot models had a four-speed pre-selective gearbox.

56C: **Triumph** Southern Cross was the company's first proper sports car and first of many Triumphs to be powered by a Coventry Climax-designed inlet-over-exhaust engine. A genuine 70 mph from its modest 1122-cc (63 × 90 mm) 33·2-bhp engine and sensible ratios in the four-speed gearbox enabled a team of these cars to win the 1934 Alpine Trial. Shown is a surviving four-seater two-door Sports tourer which in May 1933 cost £225 (Chassis £165, Coupé £260).

56D: **Vauxhall** Light Six came in two types, the 12 HP Model ASY and the 14 HP Model ASX. Both had a six-cylinder OHV engine with 100-mm stroke. Cylinder bore was 57 and 61·5 mm respectively, giving 1531- and 1781-cc cubic capacity. Sales figures of 8227 and 15,071 respectively during 1933 and 1934 proved that the 14 HP was the more popular. In fact, in 1933 Vauxhalls accounted for some 40% of all British registrations of 14 HP cars.

57A: **Wolseley** offered Hornet 12 HP, Sixteen and 21/60 models. Shown is the Hornet, which, like all other models, had a six-cylinder engine with overhead camshaft. In the case of the Hornet it had a cubic capacity of 1271 cc (57 × 83 mm). With Saloon bodywork it cost £198 10s.

57B: **Wolseley** Hornet Special was a twin-carburettor variant of the standard Hornet and was available only in chassis form, for £175. Its engine developed 40 bhp at 5000 rpm, compared with 35 at 4500 for the standard model. Both had 7 ft 6½ in wheelbase. Car shown features Trinity body by Meredith of Birmingham.

57C: **Wolseley** 21/60 was available with two wheelbase sizes, 9 ft 9 in and 10 ft 7 in. Both had a 2677-cc six-cylinder OHC engine, rated at 20·93 HP. The four-speed gearbox had a lockable freewheel. Illustrated is a Drophead Coupé on the short chassis. It had hydraulic brakes and 5.50-18 tyres. The long-wheelbase chassis had vacuum-servo brakes and 6.00-20 tyres. Note direction indicators, located in centre of front bumper. This was the first year for Wolseleys to have their traditional illuminated radiator badge.

57B Wolseley Hornet Special

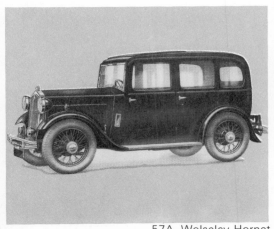

57A Wolseley Hornet

57C Wolseley 21/60

1934 In 1934 the total number of motor vehicles in use in the United Kingdom rose to 1,841,289; the following year it would pass the two million mark. Of the 1934 figure 1,333,590 units were private cars. The number of 'hackneys' rose by only 95 compared with the previous year and their total number did not change appreciably until the end of the Second World War. During the 1934 calendar year, ending in September, the British motor industry produced 342,499 vehicles of all types, of which 256,866 were cars and taxicabs. This was the highest figure so far, yet it was a far cry from the United States where manufacturers were grumbling because they had not sold more than 2¾ million vehicles, which was considerably more than all the vehicles existing in the United Kingdom. UK car exports in 1934 amounted to 43,907 units, valued at over £5·6 million. Car imports were high this year, with 10,851 units, valued at just under £1·7 million. New car registrations during the 1934 calendar year amounted to 230,866 (total of all types of new vehicles registered: 358,387).

58B   AC Ace 16/56

58A   AC 16/56

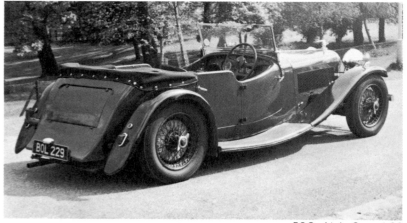

58C   Alvis Speed 20

58A: **AC** (Acedes) produced a range of 2-Litre models, all with 9 ft 7 in wheelbase. The 1990-cc (65 × 100 mm) OHC six-cylinder engine came in two variants, viz. the 16/56 (56 bhp at 3500 rpm) and the three-carburettor 16/66 (66 bhp at 3500 rpm). Both engines had a treasury rating of 15·7 HP and an aluminium cylinder block with inserted sleeves. Chassis prices were £320 and £365 respectively. Shown is a 16/56 Greyhound Saloon with sliding roof.

58B: **AC** Ace 16/56 Drophead Coupé was one of five models available and cost £435.
58C: **Alvis** SB Speed 20 Tourer. The bodywork for this and many other Alvis cars was supplied by Cross and Ellis. Shown is a preserved 1933/34 specimen belonging to a member of the Alvis Owner Club, Mr. D. H. Walters.

59A : **Armstrong Siddeley** period advertisement. The Twelve shown had a 1434-cc (56·5 × 95·25 mm) six-cylinder side-valve engine and 8 ft 9 in wheelbase. All models (12, 15, Long 15, 20, Long 20 and Siddeley Special) had four-speed self-changing gearbox.

59B : **Austin** Seven Model B9 Saloon with sliding roof (£128) contrasting sharply with its 'Mini' descendant (£533) of almost three decades later. This was one of the last 'upright' Sevens. New models with sloping radiator cowl and modernized bodywork were introduced in July.

First and still the best

ONE morning in 1928 British motorists suddenly learned that a great manufacturer was offering them for the first time the smoothness, solidity and quietness of a large and costly six in the form of a light car of moderate cost.

The new car was the Armstrong Siddeley Twelve.

Since then the same model has been constantly developed and improved. To-day it represents the most comfortable, dependable, easy to drive, simple-to-manage family car of its type. And its quality and standing have always been maintained in keeping with its proud position as pioneer and leader of the Twelve h.p. class.

COACHBUILT FAMILY SALOON £300

with the only proved self-changing gear

Write for Catalogue "H.480."

ARMSTRONG

SIDDELEY

LONDON
10, Old Bond Street, W.1

COVENTRY
Parkside

MANCHESTER
35, King Street West

Agents in all principal centres

BP480

59A Armstrong Siddeley Twelve

59B Austin Seven

1934

60A: **Austin** Ten-Four Model GRA, had not changed much since its introduction in 1932. Detail improvements included a cross-braced frame, synchro-mesh on third and top gears, electric fuel gauge and trafficator switch on steering column. The 1125-cc (63·5 × 89 mm) engine produced 20 bhp (30 bhp in Sports model). Prices ranged from £158 to £215. There were six body styles to choose from, including an attractive Cabriolet at £178.

60B: **Austin** Light Twelve Tourer, Model HT, had four-cylinder side-valve engine of 1535-cc (69·3 × 89 mm) capacity, rated at 11·9 HP. Gearbox was four-speed with synchromesh on third and top, wheelbase 8 ft 10 in, tyres 4.75-19. This model sold at £172 10s. Other body styles, selling at up to £218, were available.

60C-D: **Austin** Twenty came in two versions, the Whitehall five-seater and the Ranelagh seven-seater (shown). Wheelbase was 10 ft and 11 ft 4 in respectively, prices were £515 and £595. Both were powered by a 3·4-litre side-valve Six of 57·5 bhp, rated at 23·4 HP.

60A Austin Ten-Four

60B Austin Light Twelve

60C Austin Twenty

60D Austin Twenty

61A: **Bentley** 3½-Litre period advertisement. These fine cars were available in chassis form at £1100 for specialist coachwork but also complete as Saloon (shown) for £1460, Drophead Coupé for £1485 and Open Tourer for £1380.

61B: **British Salmson** Aero Engines Ltd. of Raynes Park, London, launched their 12/55 Model in 1934 and continued it basically unchanged until 1938. It had a 1480-cc (69 × 98 mm) 55-bhp twin-OHC four-cylinder engine, rated at 11·9 HP. The four-door Saloon shown cost £395.

61C: **BSA** built only 9·8 HP ('10') models. The 8 ft 1½ in wheelbase chassis cost £180 and the factory offered six complete Saloon and Coupé models, ranging in price from £230 to £290. Unusual for such small cars was that all had Daimler Fluid Flywheel self-changing transmission.

It is a thoroughbred vehicle, made by a firm that is famed throughout the world for the production of *the* finest car, that will trickle along in top gear at three miles an hour, and then, without protest from the engine, go straight to 80 miles an hour and better with the accelerator pedal banged down hard on the floor-boards. I know of no other sports car that will do that. The car holds the road really well at high road speeds, particularly at corners, but is without the harshness one expects to find at low speeds. I tested this over a piece of stone-paved road that is worse than any French pavé I know, with absolute success. It is a really comfortable car for both driver and passenger alike.

The Daily Herald

BENTLEY
The Silent Sports Car

BENTLEY MOTORS (1931) LTD.

16 · CONDUIT · ST · LONDON · W·I · TELEPHONE · MAYFAIR · 4412

61A   Bentley 3½-Litre

B.S.A '10'
SALOONS FROM £230

"I am delighted with the car, both in appearance and smooth and easy driving." D.M.B.

61C BSA 10

61B British Salmson 12/55

62A Crossley Torquay Ten

62A : **Crossley** offered four- and six-cylinder models ranging from the 9·8 HP Quicksilver up to the 20·9 HP Super Six. Shown is the Torquay Ten Saloon of the former series. Most expensive in the Crossley range was the Super Six Enclosed Landaulette, at £895.

62B : **Crossley** produced a limited number of this unconventional car: the Burney-designed Streamline Crossley. It had the 1991-cc 15·7 HP OHV four-cylinder engine of the 2-litre and Silver models, mounted at the rear, and independent suspension all round. All passengers sat within the 8 ft 9 in wheelbase. The car had an ENV self-changing gearbox. Previously, cars of this design had been produced by Streamline Cars Ltd., at Maidenhead, Berkshire, with a variety of engine types and longer wheelbase.

62B Crossley Streamline

63A Ford V8 Imperial

63B Ford Model 40

63C Ford Model Y

63A: **Ford** V8 Model 18 was basically similar to the Model B except that it had the American type eight-cylinder engine of 3622-cc (77·787 × 95·25 mm) capacity, rated at 30 HP. External distinguishing features were V8 ornaments on headlamp tie bar and wheel hub covers. Late production cars differed from 1932 models in having restyled wings, etc. (see 1933). Model shown was a relatively rare 10 ft 3 in wheelbase £395 Imperial Limousine, delivered to the British Army who specified oversize tyres on disc wheels.

63B: **Ford** Model 40. Whilst the British Ford Motor Company continued producing the (slightly restyled) four-cylinder Model B and BF cars, the V8s they supplied during 1933-34 were of the American Model 40 variety. The main exception was the V8 Imperial Limousine (*q.v.*) and to make matters even more complicated, the Model 40 Roadster shown, with mid-1934 Cornwall registration, had a four-cylinder engine. In the USA the Model 40 had been available with the Four engine during 1933 but because of dismal sales it was dropped there for the 1934 selling season.

63C: **Ford** Model Y Saloons were available as Tudor or 'Single Entrance' two-door at £120 and as Fordor or 'Double Entrance' four-door (illustrated) at £125. The L-head Four engine was of 933-cc capacity (56·6 × 92·5 mm) and developed 22 bhp at 3700 rpm. Treasury or RAC rating was 7·96 HP. Except for the louvres in the bonnet side panels the Model Y looked very much like the American 1933/34 Ford V8 Model 40.

63D: **Ford** Model Y chassis was available at £97 10s for the mounting of special bodywork as exemplified by this surviving 'Kerry' Tourer, which features a non-original bumper and some other modifications.

63D Ford Model Y

1934

64A : **Ford** Model Y remained in production until 1937 and from 1935 was known as Popular. By 1936 the price of the Tudor had dropped to the £100 mark, albeit after the car had been given more austere finish and equipment. These 1934/35 cars were illustrated in a 1936 issue of the Ford Times, captioned 'Thanks to the many virtues of our £100 Saloon, we are now able to forget household worries while enjoying the charm of the English countryside, at least two or three afternoons every week'.

64B : **Hillman** Minx was mechanically similar to its 1933 predecessors except that it now had a four-speed gearbox. Radiator grille, wings and bodywork were slightly restyled. Shown here with his Melody Minx Saloon are Hughie Green and his Gang outside Broadcasting House after a rehearsal for their show in the Entertainment Hour on 4 July 1934.

64C : **Hillman** Minx. These two Tourers were used by Captain and Mrs. A. E. Kellet for an arduous trip from London to Cape Town. For the expedition the cars were specially modified to carry extra petrol, water, etc. The route was via Italy, Tripolitania and Egypt.

64A Ford Model Y

64B Hillman Minx

64C Hillman Minx

65A : **Hillman** Minx Club Saloon was an attractive semi-sporting model. It sold at £195 and was one of eight models available in the Minx range.
65B : **Hillman** Minx Foursome Drophead Coupé, priced at £225, was most expensive Minx model, but the roomy locker at the rear simplified the problem of transporting tea-making equipment.
65C : **Hillman** Aero Minx was available with four different and attractive body styles. Shown are a Foursome Coupé with sliding roof and a Tourer, which were both priced at £225.
65D : **Hillman** Aero Minx cars, delivered to the Caernarvonshire Constabulary. They were used for patrol duties.

65A Hillman Minx

65C Hillman Aero Minx

65B Hillman Minx

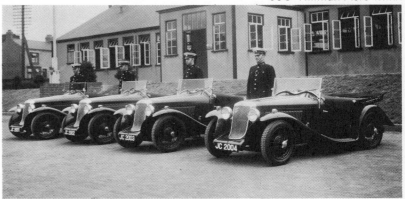

65D Hillman Aero Minx

66 Hillman 20/70

66 : **Hillman** 20/70 was similar to the Hillman 16 HP and sold at the same price (Family Saloon as shown £269). The difference was that it had the ex-Wizard 75 2810-cc (75 × 106 mm) engine, rated at 20·9 HP, rather than the 1932–33 65-mm bore Wizard 65 2210-cc unit which powered the 16 HP. The Wizards had not proved a success and were withdrawn from the Company's production programme.

67A : **Hillman** 20/70 Tourers with 68-bhp 2810-cc engines for military use, shown before delivery from the company's Coventry works.

67B : **Hillman** 20/70 Seven-seater Limousine had 10 ft 3 in wheelbase. An example is shown here at the famous Blacksmith Shop and Marriage Room at Gretna Green.

67C : **Humber** Twelve had a four-cylinder side-valve engine of 1669-cc cubic capacity (69·5 × 110 mm), rated at 11·98 HP. Power output was 42 bhp at 3800 rpm. The Sports Tourer illustrated sold at £285 and like the standard Saloon (£265) featured the early style radiator grille and louvred bonnet side panels.

67A Hillman 20/70

67B Hillman 20/70

67C Humber Twelve

1934

68A: **Humber** Twelve Vogue Saloon differed from other Twelves mainly in having bonnet ventilating doors like the bigger Humbers and special 'hardtop' bodywork, designed in collaboration with Captain Molyneux, M.C., of London and Paris. It sold at £335.

68B-C: **Humber** Twelve Sports Saloon, priced at £320, shared front end styling with Vogue model. Its body styling was particularly attractive.

68A   Humber Twelve

68B   Humber Twelve

68C   Humber Twelve

69A Humber 16/60

69B Humber Snipe

69A : **Humber** 16/60 Foursome Drophead Coupé. This bodywork was available on the Snipe 80 chassis also. Prices were £495 and £535 respectively. The 16/60 and Snipe 80 chassis were identical in most respects, main differences being in engine size (2276 and 3498·5 cc, 55 and 77·8 bhp resp.) and tyre size (6.50-18 and 6.50-17 resp.).

69B : **Humber** Snipe 80 was available with six different body styles, as well as in chassis form (£345) for the mounting of special bodies. The six-cylinder side-valve engine had a bore and stroke of 80 × 116 mm and was rated at 23·8 HP.

69C : **Humber** Snipe 80 Sports Saloon, costing £550, was acquired by explorer Rosita Forbes in preparation for a 20,000-mile journey through North, Central and South America.

69C Humber Snipe

1934

70A Humber Snipe

70B Humber Pullman

70A : **Humber** Four-light Saloon, available on 16/60 and Snipe 80 (shown) chassis, priced at £450 and £490 respectively.

70B : **Humber** Pullman was mechanically similar to the Snipe 80, featuring the same 77·8-bhp 23·8 HP 3·5-litre engine. The wheelbase, however, was one foot longer at 11 ft. This Sedanca De Ville cost £895 and had coachwork by Thrupp & Maberly. It was owned by Geraldo of the Gaucho Tango Orchestra (Savoy Hotel, London).

70C : **Humber** Pullman with Thrupp & Maberly Sedanca Coupé bodywork. This 4/5-seater model had a three-way folding top, easily adaptable as an open Sports Tourer, or Semi-closed Coupé as shown.

70C Humber Pullman

71A Jowett 4G

71B: **Lagonda** Rapier 10 HP chassis was introduced in late 1933 and continued in production for only a few years. It had an 1104-cc (62·5 × 90 mm) twin-OHC four-cylinder engine, developing 60 bhp at 5000 rpm and rated at 9·69 HP. The four-speed gearbox had right hand control. The wheelbase was 8 ft 4 in, the tyre size 4.50-19. Car shown has Fixed-head Coupé body by Abbott.

71C: **Lagonda** Rapier Four-seater Tourer by Abbott. This was the most common body style on the Rapier, which was only supplied in chassis form by the factory.

71D: **Lagonda** offered six-cylinder 16/80 Special Six, 3-Litre and 4½-Litre models, in addition to the Rapier Four. Both the 3- and 4½-Litre chassis had 10 ft 9 in wheelbase and 6.00-19 tyres. The 3-Litre had a 79-bhp 3181-cc OHV engine, rated at 29·94 HP. The 4½-Litre, a preserved Tourer model of which is illustrated here, had a 29·13 HP 4429-cc OHV Six with an output of 104 bhp at 3000 rpm. The Tourer, when new, cost £825. Note the 'cycle wings'.

71B Lagonda Rapier

71C Lagonda Rapier

71A: **Jowett** produced two types of chassis, the 4G Short (wb 7 ft) and 4G Long (wb 8 ft 6 in). Mechanically they were similar, featuring the legendary 907-cc (75·4 × 101·6 mm) side-valve flat-twin engine which was rated at 7·04 HP. Actual power output was 16 bhp at 3000 rpm. Gearbox was four-speed, tyre size 4.50-19. The two chassis were available at £109 10s and £111 10s respectively, complete cars costing from £151 up to £175 ex-works.

71D Lagonda 4½-Litre

72A: **Lagonda** 4½-Litre M45; another beautifully preserved Tourer model of this sturdy sports car, photographed at Silverstone in April, 1968. The Lagonda M45 Rapide was a higher-performance version. Power output was 104 bhp at 3000 rpm and 120 bhp at 3200 rpm respectively.

72B: **Lanchester**, like Daimler, was a member of the BSA group of Companies. The company offered lines of 10 and 18 HP models with four- and six-cylinder engines respectively, both featuring the Daimler Fluid Flywheel self-changing gearbox. The 10 HP shown in this period advertisement stood on an 8 ft 6⅝ in wheelbase chassis with 5.00-18 tyres and conventional semi-elliptic leaf springs. The chassis was available for £245.

72C: **Morgan** offered a wide range of three-wheeled models, priced from £105 to £135, with 990- and 1100-cc engines, all of the V-twin-cylinder type. All of the nine 1934 models had 9 ft 3 in wheelbase and 18 × 3 Dunlop Magna wheels. Two had air-cooled engines and three of the water-cooled types had side valves. Shown is a Super Sports model with Matchless water-cooled OHV engine which was extensively rebuilt thirty years later.

72D: **Morris** Minor Tourer cost £120 and was cheapest but one of the smallest of 1934 Morrises. Full range comprised 32 basic models in eight series, viz. Minor, Ten Four, Ten Six, Cowley, Cowley Six, Oxford, Isis and 25. Minor series comprised Two-Seater, Tourer, two two-door Saloons, four-door Saloon and Special Coupé. They had an 847-cc side-valve Four engine, four-speed gearbox and hydraulic brakes. Wheelbase measured 6 ft 6 in for all except the four-door Saloon and Special Coupé which was 7 ft 7 in. Drive-away chassis were available at £92 10s and £102 10s respectively.

72A Lagonda 4½-Litre

72B Lanchester 10 HP

72C Morgan Super Sports

72D Morris Minor

73A Morris Ten Six

73C Morris 25 Six

73B Morris Cowley Six

73D Morris Eight

73A: **Morris** Ten Six Special Coupé was new for 1934. Two-seater, Tourer, and Saloon body styles were offered also. Engine was a six-cylinder side-valve unit of 1378-cc capacity (57 × 90 mm), rated at 12 HP. Apart from engine, gearbox ratios and 6-in shorter wheelbase the Ten Four models were very similar. The Special Coupé shown cost £215 as Ten Six, £200 as Ten Four.

73B: **Morris** Cowley Six was a new addition to the range. The existing Cowley Four was improved and had a new engine. Except for the £265 Six Special Coupé all Cowleys had four-door Saloon bodywork. The Six Saloon with sliding roof cost £220, the fixed-roof edition was £5 cheaper. The Cowley Six engine had 63·5 × 102 mm bore and stroke (1938 cc), the Four had 6-mm larger bore and same stroke (1550 cc). Both had 5.00-19 tyres. Wheelbase was 8 ft 10 in and 8 ft 6 in respectively.

73C: **Morris** 25 featured 'single-pedal control' for normal driving, provided by free-wheel and Bendix automatic clutch control. Either or both could be put out of action by a dash-mounted control. The 25 had a side-valve six-cylinder engine of 3485-cc capacity (82 × 110 mm). Morris' other 'Big Sixes' were the 2062-cc side-valve Oxford Six and the 2468-cc overhead-valve Isis Six. The 25 Saloon shown cost £395, incl. sliding roof.

73D: **Morris** Minor was restyled and enlarged in the summer of 1934, for the 1935 model year, and the new model was designated Eight (Eight Series I from mid-1935). Several body styles were available, the £120 Tourer being particularly popular. Shown is the 5-cwt Van variant. Engine and gearbox now were 918-cc (57 × 90 mm) and three-speed respectively. Wheelbase was increased from 6 ft 6 in to 7 ft 6 in and track from 3 ft 6 in to 3 ft 9 in. Later they became known as the 'Pre-Series' models.

1934

74A Railton Open Sports

74B Railton Sports Saloon

74A: **Railton** cars were built, from 1933, by Railton Cars, at Fairmile Engineering (the old Invicta works), Cobham in Surrey. They consisted of a sturdy 9 ft 8 in wheelbase chassis with, from mid-1934, a Hudson straight-eight side-valve engine of 4168-cc capacity, developing 113 bhp at 3800 rpm and rated at 28·8 HP. Drive to the 4·11:1 rear axle was through a three-speed gearbox. The wire wheels were fitted with 6.25-16 Air Wheel tyres. The chassis cost £430, the Open Sports model shown £540.

74B: **Railton** Two-door Sports Saloon was offered at £630 and was most expensive of the range. Other models included a Four-door Saloon and a Drophead Coupé, selling at £565 and £595 respectively.

74C: **Riley** six-cylinder chassis with Gamecock body and cycle wings. Six-cylinder chassis were available with 1458-cc 12·08 HP and 1633-cc 13·53 HP engine with brake horse-power outputs from 44 to 57, depending on specification. All had overhead valves and four-speed gearbox.

74C Riley Gamecock

75A: **Riley** Nine was available with seven factory-built body styles, ranging in price from £237 to £325. Shown is the £325 Kestrel Saloon with 'fastback'. The engine was an OHV Four of 1098-cc capacity (60·3 × 95·2 mm), rated at 9·02 HP and developing 35 bhp at 4500 rpm. Most models were optionally available with a less powerful version, developing 27 bhp at 4000 rpm.

75B: **Rolls-Royce** 20/25 chassis with Sports Saloon coachwork by Barker. Engine was 3669-cc (82 × 114 mm) OHV Six of 25·3 HP, chassis price £1050. Also available was 7668-cc (108 × 140 mm) 43·3 HP LWB chassis, Model 40/50.

75C: **Rover** Twelve was a new car, available in Chassis, Saloon (shown), Open Four-Seater and Sports Saloon form at £195, £278, £288 and £298 respectively. Engine was an 11·9 HP overhead-valve 1485-cc (69 × 100 mm) Four, with four-speed gearbox, featuring clutchless gear-change and free-wheel.

75A Riley Nine Kestrel

75B Rolls-Royce 20/25

75C Rover Twelve

76A Singer Nine Le Mans

76B Singer Eleven Airstream

76A: **Singer** Le Mans Two-seater was one of a wide range of models in Singer's Nine series. All Nines had a 972-cc (60 × 86 mm) OHC engine, rated at 8·93 HP. Actual brake horse-power depended on model. The Le Mans Two-seater had a 34-bhp power unit, the Le Mans Speed model a 38-bhp. At the lower end of the range were 26·5- and 28-bhp engines. Le Mans models had twin carburettors. Car shown is taking part in the Lawrence Cup Trial, after having competed in the Scottish Rally.

76B: **Singer** Eleven (10·5 HP) series comprised five models, including this unusual Airstream Saloon which sold at £300. It featured built-in headlamps and clutchless gear change (Fluidrive). All Eleven models had 8 ft 4 in wheelbase and 1384-cc (65 × 105 mm) OHC engine of 35 bhp, except the Sports Saloon which had a 40-bhp variant. Shown with the Airstream is Jack Payne, the dance band leader. He liked the car and bought 14, all the same colour, for the members of the band.

76C: **SS** Cars Limited offered 10, 12, 16 and 20 HP models with Tourer and Saloon body styles, priced from £260 for the SS II 10 HP Tourer up to £365 for the SS I 20 HP Airline Saloon.

76C SS I

77A: **Standard** Ten-Twelve Speed Saloon was powered by a twin-carburettor 1608-cc (69·5 × 106 mm) side-valve engine with an output of 45 bhp at 4000 rpm. It was rated at 11·98 HP and sold at £245. The chassis was available for special bodywork at £180. Tyre size was 4.75-17, wheelbase 7 ft 10 in.

77B: **Standard** Ten succeeded the Big Nine and had increased piston stroke (106 vs. 101·6 mm; bore remained 63·5 mm). It had 7 ft 10 in wheelbase and 4.50-18 tyres on big-hub wire wheels. The chassis price was £130; complete cars cost £168 to £192.

77C: **Sunbeam** Twenty-Five with a difference. This 1934 chassis was rebodied in 1937 by Thrupp & Maberly and belonged to H.R.H. The Duke of Gloucester. The limousine was painted in the royal colours and intended specially for use on State occasions.

77D: **Talbot** Sixty-Five Special Coachbuilt Saloon was one of three models available on 9 ft 6 in wheelbase chassis with 45-bhp 1666-cc (61 × 95 mm) 13·8 HP OHV six-cylinder engine. Like all other 1934 Talbots it had a pre-selective four-speed gearbox. Model shown cost £425.

77B Standard Ten

77A Standard Ten-Twelve Speed

77C Sunbeam Twenty-Five

77D Talbot Sixty-Five Special

78A Talbot Seventy-Five

78B: **Talbot** 105 Sports Four-door Saloon was a high-performance car, offered at £795. It had the same wheelbase as the 65 and the SWB 75, namely 9 ft 6 in, and basically the same engine as the Talbot 95: a 2970-cc (75 × 112 mm) OHV Six, rated at 20·9 HP. Brake horsepower figures for the 95 and 105 were 95 and 100 respectively, both at 4500 rpm.
78C: **Talbot** 105 chassis was available for mounting bodywork to customer's choice. Shown is a two-door four-seater Tourer which took part in the 1934 Welsh Rally.

78A: **Talbot** Seventy-Five chassis cost £395 with 9 ft 6 in, £425 with 10 ft wheelbase. The engine was a 17·9 HP 2276-cc (69·5 × 100 mm) OHV unit, developing 70 bhp at 4500 rpm. Coachbuilt Saloons on these two chassis were priced £495 and £545 respectively.

78B Talbot 105

78C Talbot 105

79A: **Talbot** 105 in Brooklands guise. These cars, with 'authentic replica body', had outstanding successes on road and track.

79B: **Triumph** Gloria Saloon was one of a wide range of new 9·53 HP models introduced for the 1934 season. Bore and stroke of the four-cylinder inlet-over-exhaust valve engines were 62 × 90 mm (1807 cc) but power output varied from 33½ bhp at 4300 rpm up to 46 at 4600, depending on model.

79C: **Vauxhall** Light Six A-Series 12 HP chassis with Drophead Coupé bodywork. The chassis, Model ASY, cost £140 and had a 36-bhp 1531-cc (57 × 100 mm) OHV six-cylinder engine. Much the same chassis was available with 61·5-mm bore (14 HP) engine, developing 42 bhp, designated Model ASX. Both had 8 ft 5 in wheelbase and 4.75-17 tyres.

79D: **Vauxhall** Big Six B-Series comprised three basic types, viz. the 19·8 HP BY and the 26·3 HP BX and BXL. The latter had 10 ft 10 in wheelbase, the others 9 ft 3 in. The 19·8 (20) HP engine was a 53-bhp OHV 2·4-Litre unit, the 26·3 (26) HP was a larger-bore 3·2-Litre variant developing 64 bhp. Both had a four-speed gearbox and automatic chassis lubrication. The Model BY Saloon shown cost £325.

79A Talbot 105

79B Triumph 9·53 HP Gloria

79C Vauxhall Light Six

79D Vauxhall Big Six

INDEX

SUMMARY OF MAJOR BRITISH CAR MAKES
1930-1934 (with dates of their existence)

AC	(from 1908)	Morgan	(from 1910)
Alvis	(1920–67)	Morris	(from 1913)
Armstrong Siddeley	(1919–60)		
Aston Martin	(from 1922)	Riley	(1898–1969)
Austin	(from 1906)		
		Rolls-Royce	(from 1904)
Bentley	(from 1920)	Rover	(from 1904)
BSA	(1933–36)		
		Singer	(1905–70)
Crossley	(1904–37)	SS (later Jaguar)	(from 1932)
		Standard	(1903–63)
Daimler	(from 1896)	Sunbeam	(1899–1937)**
		Sunbeam-Talbot	(1938–54)
Ford	(from 1911)		
Frazer-Nash	(1924–60)	Talbot	(1903–38)
		Triumph	(from 1923)
Hillman	(from 1907)	Trojan	(1922–36)
Humber	(from 1898)		
		Vauxhall	(from 1903)
Jowett	(1906–54)		
		Wolseley	(from 1911)
Lagonda	(1906–63)		
Lanchester	(1895–1956)		
Lea-Francis	(1904–60)*	*irregularly	
MG	(from 1924)	**and from 1953	

ACKNOWLEDGEMENTS

This book was compiled and written largely from historical source material in the library of the Olyslager Organisation, and in addition photographs and/or other material was kindly provided or loaned by several manufacturers and other organizations, notably

AC Cars Ltd, Alvis Ltd, Alvis Owner Club (Mr. R. A. Cox), British Leyland Motor Corp. Ltd, British Salmson Owner's Club (Mr. P. A. M. Perry), Chrysler United Kingdom Ltd, Devon Vintage Car Club (Mr. D. K. Myers), Dorking Motor Company Ltd, Ford Motor Company Ltd, Jaguar Cars Ltd, Morgan Motor Company Ltd, The National Motor Museum, Old Motor Magazine, The Rover Company Ltd, The Society of Motor Manufacturers and Traders Ltd, Triumph Motor Company Ltd, Triumph Owners Club (Mr. A. C. Cook), Vauxhall Motors Ltd, and Wadham Stringer (Guildford) Ltd, as well as a number of private individuals, particularly Messrs. L. W. Barr, G. A. Ingram and D. Lipscombe.

The Editor's special thanks are due to Michael Sedgwick, David J. Voller, John M. Carpenter and Dick Schornagel for valuable assistance rendered in collating and checking material.